MW00603879

Retro
Kitchen
KNITS

Printed in the United States of America

Second Printing, 2015

978-1-62767-042-5

Versa Press, Inc
800-447-7829

www.versapress.com

CONTENTS

Bread Warmer 4

Chevron Mason Jar 8

Dappled Lace Cafe Curtains 12

Eyelet Lace Mason Jar Cozy 16

Gingham Towl Set 20

Pot Grabber 24

Seed Stitch Rug 28

BREAD WARMER

by Kerin Dimeler-Laurence

FINISHED MEASUREMENTS
20" square

YARN
Knit Picks CotLin (70% Tanguis Cotton, 30% Linen; 123 yards/50g): MC Raindrop 25326, CC Swan 24134, 2 balls each.

NEEDLES
US 5 (3.75 mm) 24" circular needles, or size to obtain gauge

NOTIONS
Tapestry Needle
Stitch Holder or Scrap Yarn
Stitch Markers

GAUGE
23 sts and 40 rows = 4" in Seed Stitch, blocked.
23 sts and 44 rows = 4" In Mosaic pattern, blocked.

Bread Warmer

Notes:

Mosaic and seed stitch combine to give a beautiful and functional setting for your baked goods.

Seed Stitch

Worked flat, over an even number of sts.

Row 1: *K1, P1. Repeat from * to end of row.

Row 2: *P1, K1. Repeat from * to end of row.

Repeat rows 1 and 2 for pattern.

Make 1 (M1)

PU the bar between st just worked and next st and place on LH needle mounted as a regular stitch; knit through the back of the loop.

Mosaic stitch in the round

Each row of the mosaic chart represents two rounds, knit with one color at a time. To work the first round of the pair, knit the stitches that appear on the chart in your current color, and slip those in the other color to the RH needle with yarn held in back. To work the second round of the pair, purl the stitches that appear on the chart in your current color, and slip those in the other color to the RH needle with yarn held in back. Each round of the chart is read from right to left.

Mosaic Increases

Increases at the corners happen on the first row of each 'pair' of rows. When you come to a corner stitch, (M1, knit corner st, M1) in current color. On the second round, purl these three sts as usual.

DIRECTIONS

A pocket in this cloth holds a clay tablet or buckwheat pillow that keeps your bread out-of-the-oven warm. The cloth and pocket are worked in Seed stitch, and a border is picked up and worked in reversible Mosaic stitch.

With MC Raindrop, CO 100 sts. Work in Seed st for 2.5".

On the next row, set aside stitches for the pocket: Work in Seed st for 67 sts. Place the last 34 sts worked onto scrap yarn or a stitch holder; continue working the remaining 33 sts in Seed st.

On the next row, work 33 sts in Seed St, CO 34 sts, and join to live sts at the other side; continue across row. Work in Seed st until piece measures 17" long.

Border

On the next row, set up for the border: Knit across all 100 sts, *PM, PU and K 1 st in the corner, PU and K 100 sts across the adjacent side,* repeat between *s twice more. 404 sts on the needles. Join to work in the round and purl one round.

Attach CC. Knit one round, then purl one round.

Begin working from Mosaic Border chart around all sts. After last round of chart, (knit one round, purl one round) in CC, break CC then knit one round in MC; BO all sts.

Pocket

Place 34 held sts on the needles. With MC, CO 1 st to the right of the first live st, leaving a long tail; work across 35 sts in Seed st as established, CO 1 st at the end. 36 sts on the needles.

Work in Seed st for 12". Break yarn, leaving a tail of 5-6'. With a yarn needle, graft the live sts to the body on the underside (wrong side of Mosaic pattern would be showing) of the bread warmer, lining the pocket up with beginning sts. Whipstitch up the adjacent side to the opening of the pocket. Using the yarn tail from the pocket cast on, whipstitch the pocket flap to the body on the other long edge.

Finishing

Weave in ends, wash and block.

Mosaic Border

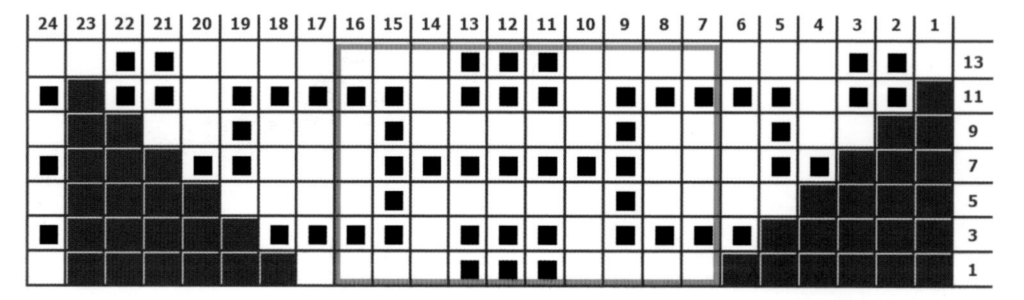

CHEVRON MASON JAR COZY

by Jenny Konopinski

FINISHED MEASUREMENTS
8.5 (10.5)" circumference, 3 (4)" tall

YARN
Knit Picks Curio (100% Cotton; 721 yards/100g): Sagebrush 26267, 1 ball

NEEDLES
US 1 (2.5mm) DPNs or two 24" circular needles for two circulars technique, or one 32" or longer circular needle for Magic Loop technique, or size to obtain gauge

NOTIONS
Stitch Markers
Tapestry Needle
8oz Mason Jar (to fit small cozy)
16oz Mason Jar (to fit large cozy)

GAUGE
23.5 sts and 40 rows = 4" over lace patterns, blocked and stretched.

Chevron Mason Jar Cozy

Notes:
Worked in the round from the top down, use these charming Mason jar cozies to add splashes of color to your home and kitchen.

SK2P
Slip 1 stitch, K2tog, pass slipped stitch over. 2 sts dec.

Follow the chart from bottom to top, reading each round from right to left as a RS row.

Chevron Pattern (worked in the round over a multiple of 10 sts)
Round 1: k5, yo, ssk, k3
Round 2, 4, 6, 8, 10: Knit
Round 3: K3, k2tog, yo, k1, yo, ssk, k2
Round 5: K2, k2tog, yo, k3, yo, ssk, k1
Round 7: K1, k2tog, yo, k5, yo, ssk
Round 8: Knit to last stitch and move the end of round marker to the right of last stitch.
Round 9: Sk2p, yo, k7, yo

Repeat Rounds 1-10 for pattern.

DIRECTIONS

Starting from the top down, CO 50 (60) sts. PM and join to work in the round, being careful not to twist sts.

Knit 1 row.

Body

Work the Chevron Pattern a total of 5 (6) times across each row.

Complete 3 (4) full repeats of the Chevron pattern to create the body.

Base

To form the base, knit 2 rows.

Round 1: *Purl 23 (13), p2tog, rep from* 2 (4) times. 48 (56) sts.
Round 2 and following even rounds: Knit
Round 3: *K 4 (5), k2tog, rep from* 8 times. 40 (48) sts
Round 5: *K 3 (4), k2tog, rep from* 8 times. 32 (40) sts
Round 7: *K 2 (3), k2tog, rep from* 8 times. 24 (32) sts.
Round 9: *K 1 (2), k2tog, rep from * 8 times. 16 (24) sts
Round 11: Small - k2tog around; Large – *K1, k2tog, rep from* 8 times. 8 (16) sts
Round 13: K2tog around. 4 (8) sts
Round 15: Large only - K2tog around. 4 sts

Finishing

Cut yarn leaving a 6" tail. Weave through remaining 4 sts and pull closed. Weave in ends.

Wet block the cozy and place it over the Mason jar. Turn upside down and let air dry.

You can use a rubber band to secure the top of the cozy in place as it is blocking to hold the shape of the jar. The cozy will stretch to snugly fit the cozy once it is wet.

Chevron Pattern

10	9	8	7	6	5	4	3	2	1	
										10
yo								yo	sk2p	9
										8
ssk	yo						yo	k2tog		7
										6
	ssk	yo				yo	k2tog			5
										4
		ssk	yo		yo	k2tog				3
										2
			ssk	yo						1

Note: On Row 8, knit to last stitch and move the end of round marker to the right of last stitch.

Legend:

knit
knit stitch

yo
Yarn Over

ssk
Slip one stitch as if to knit, Slip another stitch as if to knit. Insert left-hand needle into front of these 2 stitches and knit them together

k2tog
Knit two stitches together as one stitch

sl1 k2tog psso
slip 1, k2tog, pass slip stitch over k2tog

DAPPLED LACE CAFÉ CURTAINS

by Knit Picks Design Team

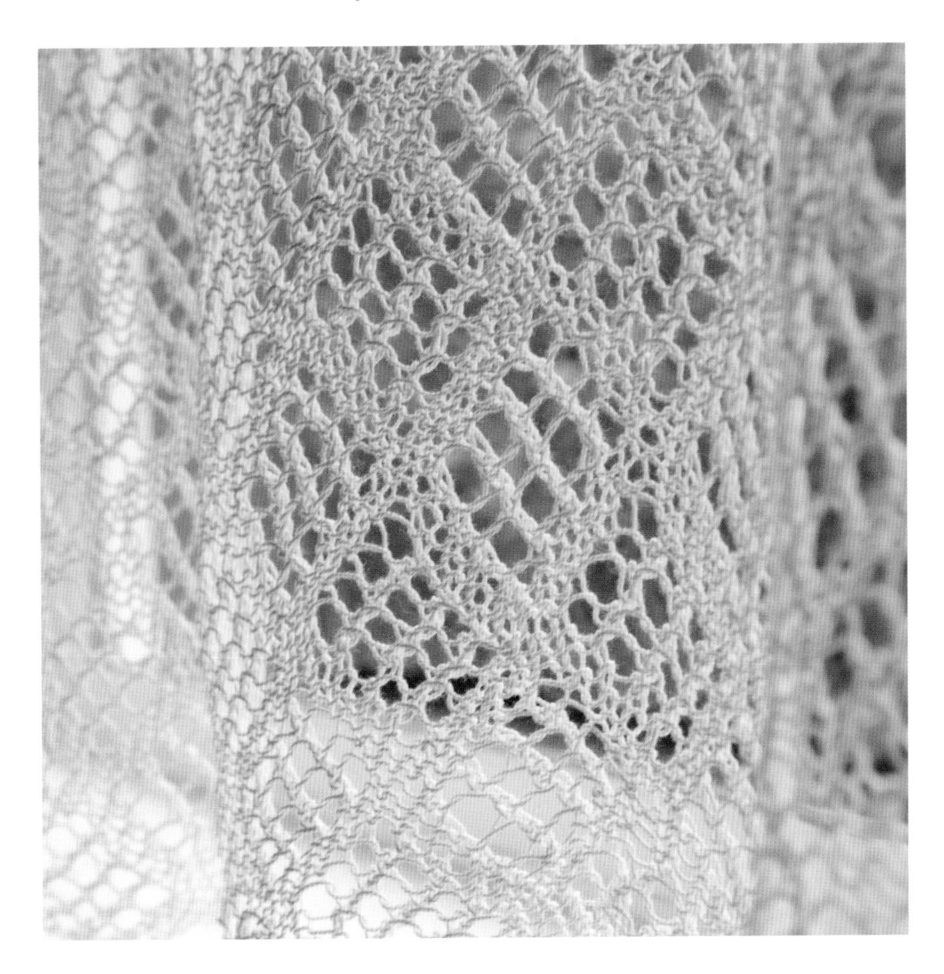

FINISHED MEASUREMENTS
Approximately 48" x 15", excluding hem

YARN
Knit Picks Curio (100% cotton; 721 yds/100 g): White 26255, 1 ball

NEEDLES
US 6 (4.0 mm): Circular or straights. If necessary, adjust needle size to obtain correct gauge.

NOTIONS
Yarn needle
Tension rod for mounting

GAUGE
16 sts/26.5 rows = 4" in Checkerboard Mesh on US6s. Check your gauge before you begin.

Dapped Lace Café Curtains

Notes:

This wavy mesh curtain offers light and privacy for your home. It can easily be made wider or longer if needed: every 10 additonal stitches equals 2½", and each vertical repeat of the pattern is about 3".

If you are feeling particularly ambitious, turn it into a bed skirt - just insert elastic into the finished hem so that it snugs up to your box spring.

A slightly loosened gauge gives the lace a more airy quality.

Checkerboard Mesh (Multiple of 10 sts + 4)
Row 1 and all WS rows: P.
Row 2 (RS): K4, *yo, ssk, k1, (k2tog, yo) twice, k3;* rep from * to *.
Row 4: *K3, (yo, ssk) twice, k1, k2tog, yo*; rep from * to *; end k4.
Row 6: K2, *(yo, ssk) 3 times, k4*; rep from * to *, end yo, ssk.
Row 8: K1, *(yo, ssk) 4 times, k2*; rep from * to *, end yo, ssk, k1.
Row 10: Rep row 6.
Row 12: Rep row 4.
Row 14: Rep row 2.
Row 16: K2tog, yo, *k4, (K2tog, yo) 3 times*; rep from * to*, end k2.
Row 18: K1, k2tog, yo; *k2, (k2tog, yo) 4 times*; rep from * to *, end k1.
Row 20: Rep row 16.
Rep rows 1-20 for pattern.

DIRECTIONS

CO 198 sts.
Row 1: Sl 1, k1; work row 1 of Checkerboard Mesh to last two sts; end k2.

Cont to work selvedge sts as given in Row 1, work five repeats of the Checkerboard Mesh pattern (piece measures approximately 15").

Changing to St st, work 12 rows for outside of hem. P 1 row (turning ridge), then work 12 more rows of stockinette for inside hem. BO loosely.

Finishing

Block curtain: in warm water, soak the curtain until it is thoroughly damp. Spread the piece across a large towel; roll the towel and curtain together and press gently to remove the water (do not wring). Remove the curtain from the roll and lay on a flat surface to dry, pinning to measurements.

When dry, fold hem at turning ridge; using whip stitch, tack the bound-off edge to the WS of the curtain, making sure to leave both ends open.

To mount, slide curtain onto a 1" tension rod and set inside window. CO 3 sts. *Knit two stitches and slip the third stitch knitwise. PU and knit one more stitch from the edge. You will now have 4 stitches on your right needle.

Use your left needle tip to pass the slipped stitch over the last knitted stitch. This will leave you with three stitches on your right needle.

Slip these three stitches back onto the left needle tip, or slide to the other end of the needle, purlwise. Tug on the working yarn to tighten up the stitches.

Repeat these steps from *.

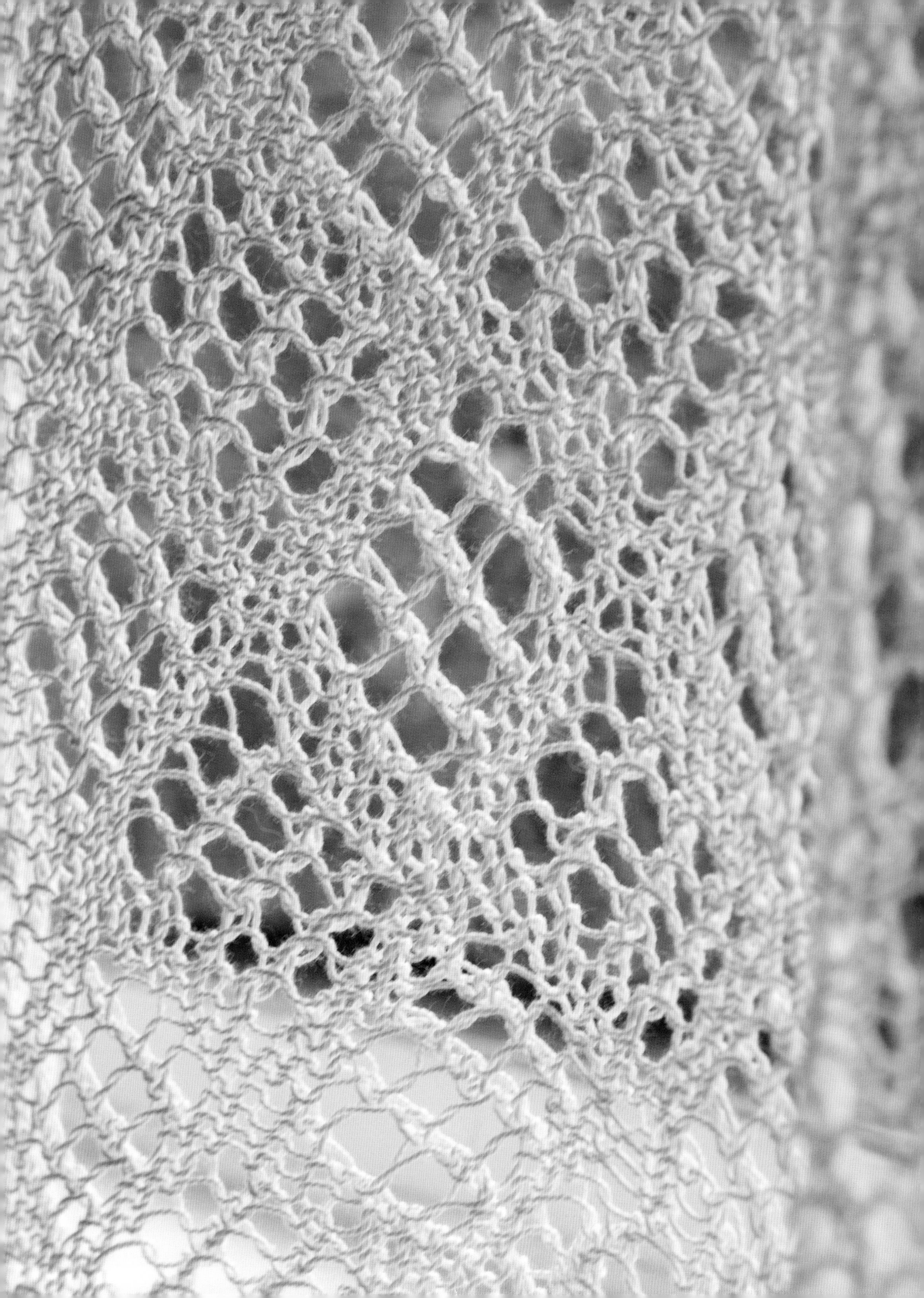

EYELET LACE MASON JAR COZY

by Alison Backus

FINISHED MEASUREMENTS
To fit a narrow-mouth pint jar, 5.5" high at collar.

YARN
Knit Picks Curio #10 Crochet Thread (100% cotton; 721 yards/100g): White 26255.

NEEDLES
US 1 (2.5mm) DPNs or circular needles, or size to obtain gauge

NOTIONS
Yarn Needle
8 Stitch Markers

GAUGE
30 sts and 48 rows = 4" in St st in the round, unstretched
22 sts and 40 rows = 4" in St st in the round, blocked and stretched on jar

Eyelet Lace Mason Jar Cozy

Notes:
Lovely and functional Mason jar cozy in easy eyelet lace stitch pattern.

Eyelet Lace Stitch Pattern (in the round over an even number of sts)
Round 1: *K2tog, yo, rep from * to end of round.
Round 2: Knit.
Repeat rounds 1 and 2 for pattern.

DIRECTIONS

The Mason jar cozy is worked from the top down.

Body

Using long tail cast on, loosely cast on 56 stitches. Join in round, PM, being careful not to twist sts.
Knit 10 rounds.
Work 3 repeats of Eyelet Lace Stitch Pattern (6 rounds).
Knit 4 rounds.
Work three repeats of Eyelet Lace Stitch Pattern (6 rounds).
Knit 4 rounds.
Work 3 repeats of Eyelet Lace Stitch Pattern. (6 rounds).
Knit 10 rounds.

Bottom

Purl 1 round.
Knit 1 round, placing markers every 7 stitches, 8 markers placed.

Decrease Round: *Knit to two stitches before marker, k2tog, rep from * around.
Next Round: Knit.

Repeat last two rounds until 8 stitches remain. Break yarn and thread through stitches, pull tight to close bottom. Weave in ends.

Finishing

Gently stretch over your mason jar. Spray water gently over the stretched jar cozy and smooth the fabric on the jar, then allow to dry completely.

GINGHAM TOWEL SET

by Kerin Dimeler-Laurence

FINISHED MEASUREMENTS
Dishcloths: 10" square
Kitchen Towels: 12x18"
Tea Towel: 15x24"

YARN
Knit Picks Dishie (100% Cotton; 190 yards/100g): Swan 25409, Conch 25411, 4 balls each.

NEEDLES
US 7 (4.5 mm) straight or circular needles, or size to obtain gauge

NOTIONS
Tapestry Needle
Stitch Markers

GAUGE
Dishcloth: 20 sts and 26 rows = 4" in Gingham Texture pattern, blocked.
Kitchen Towels: 25 sts and 29 rows = 4" in stranded Gingham patterns, blocked.
Tea Towel: 20 sts and 30 rows = 4" In Chevron pattern, blocked.

Gingham Towel Set

Notes:
This set of five towels does it all!

Garter Stitch
Knit every row.

DIRECTIONS

Dishcloths

Both of these cloths are worked the same way, each in a different color.

With Swan or Conch, CO 50 sts. Work in Garter st for 10 rows. On the next row, set up pattern: K5, PM, work from row 1 of Gingham Texture chart, repeating these ten sts four times, PM, K5.

Continue working as established, keeping the first and last 5 sts in Garter st and working from the Gingham Texture chart between markers. Repeat the 10 rows of the chart four full times, then work through row 5 once more.

Work 10 rows in Garter st. BO all sts. Weave in and secure ends. Wash and block.

Make a second cloth in the other color.

Finishing

Weave in ends, wash, block and use proudly!

Gingham Kitchen Towels

This set of two heavy-duty towels is tough, absorbent, and attractive! Though two colors are held throughout the colorwork portion, one color in each is extended into a garter stitch border, the other dropped and then picked up again when needed on the next row. If desired, tack long floats as you go. Leave long ends to weave in; with how much use these towels will get, good finishing is a must!

Diagonal Gingham Towel
With Conch, CO 70 sts. Work in Garter st for 10 rows. On the next row, set up pattern: K5, PM, attach Swan and work from row 1 of Diagonal Gingham chart, repeating these ten sts six times, PM, K5 in Conch.

Continue working as established, keeping the first and last 5 sts in Garter st with Conch and working from the Diagonal Gingham chart between markers. Repeat the 10 rows of the chart 12 full times. Break Swan.

With Conch, work 10 rows in Garter st. BO all sts.

Finishing

Weave in and secure ends. Wash and block to Finished Measurements.

Checked Gingham Towel
With Swan, CO 70 sts. Work in Garter st for 10 rows. On the next row, set up pattern: K5, PM, attach Conch and work from row 1 of Checked Gingham chart, repeating these ten sts six times, PM, K5 in Swan.

Continue working as established, keeping the first and last 5 sts in Garter st with Swan and working from the Checked Gingham chart between markers. Repeat the 10 rows of the chart 12 full times. Break Conch.

With Swan, work 10 rows in Garter st. BO all sts.

Finishing

Weave in ends, wash, block and use proudly!

Slip Stitch Tea Towel
This sweet tea towel is attractive in a guest bath, bread basket, or as the heavy duty drying towel you've been wanting in the kitchen. Two-color slip stitch forms a sturdy border, and a light-relief pattern of chevrons gives the towel just enough texture.

With Conch, CO 77 sts. Work four rows in Garter st. Attach Swan and begin working from Tea Towel chart; the repeat of the slip stitch motif is only two stitches wide, but several more repeats are shown, before rows end with one half of the slip stitch pattern and the Garter edge stitches. Work the four-row repeat of the slip stitch motif four times, changing colors as shown in chart, then continue on to row 5. After the last Garter st row on row 10, break Conch and continue in Swan.

Chevron Motif: Repeat the 14 sts of the Chevron Motif five times, then work the last seven sts of the chart. Repeat the 6 rows of the motif 21 times, then attach Conch and work rows 17 through 20 of the chart.

Work four repeats of rows 21-24, then work to the end of the chart. Break Swan. With Conch, work four rows in Garter st. BO all sts.

Finishing

Weave in ends, wash and block.

POT GRABBERS

by Kerin Dimeler-Laurence

FINISHED MEASUREMENTS

4.5 x 8.5" (makes 2)

YARN

Knit Picks CotLin (70% Tanguis Cotton, 30% Linen; 123 yards/50g): MC Swan 24134, 2 balls; CC Moroccan Red 23996, 1 ball.

NEEDLES

US 5 (3.75 mm) circular or straight needles, or size to obtain gauge

NOTIONS

Insul-Bright batting (optional)
Yarn Needle

Pot Grabbers

Notes:
These handy pot holders are designed to fit over your fingers and thumb, allowing you to easily grasp baking sheets, pots, or any other hot item.

DIRECTIONS

Each pot grabber is knit in two pieces, with an attached I-cord border around the outside. For extra insulation, add a layer of Insul-Bright batting where instructed.

Outer Pocket Layer

With Swan, and using backwards loop CO, cast on 14 sts. Knit across these sts. Turning work so that cast-on edge is on top and working yarn is to the right of the work, PU and knit into each cast-on st (including the slip knot). You are now working in the round. If using DPNs, arrange so that there are 7 sts on each of 4 needles. For two circular needles or magic loop, 14 sts should be on each side. From here, all color changes and shaping are charted.

First round (round 1 of the chart): PM to mark beginning of round. K1, M1L, K to last st of first side, M1R, K1. Repeat for second side; 4 sts increased. Repeat this increase round every round four times more, following color changes in the chart for these and all remaining rounds. 48 sts. Knit in St st for 14 rounds.

Round 20: P24, K24.
Round 21: Knit.
Round 22: P1, BO 22 P-wise, P1, K24. Begin knitting flat, knitting the remaining st from the beginning of the next round.
Row 23: K1, P24, K1.
Row 24: K 26.
Rows 25-34: Repeat rows 23-24 five times.
Row 35: K1, P24, K1.
Row 36: K 26, CO 22 sts and join in the round again. These cast on sts form a portion of the next round.
Round 37: K25 to finish the round.
Round 38: P24, K24.
Work in St st for 16 rounds.
Round 55: *SSK, K20, K2tog; repeat once more. 44 sts.
Round 56: *SSK, K18, K2tog; repeat once more. 40 sts.
Round 57: *SSK, K16, K2tog; repeat once more. 36 sts.
Round 58: *SSK, K14, K2tog; repeat once more. 32 sts.
Round 59: *SSK, K12, K2tog; repeat once more. 28 sts.
Break yarn, leaving an 18" tail of Swan. Using this tail, graft the two sides of the open end closed. Weave in ends.

Inner Layer

The inner layer provides extra protection from heat.
With Swan, CO 12 sts. Purl one row.
Row 1: K1, M1L, K10, M1R, K1. 14 sts.
Row 2: P1, M1L P-wise, P12, M1R P-wise, P1. 16 sts.
Row 3: K1, M1L, K14, M1R, K1. 18 sts.
Row 4: P1, M1L P-wise, P16, M1R P-wise, P1. 20 sts.
Row 5: K1, M1L, K18, M1R, K1. 22 sts.
Work in St st for 45 rows.
Row 51: K2tog, K to last 2 sts, SSK. 20 sts.
Row 52: SSP, P to last 2 sts, P2tog. 18 sts.
Row 53: K2tog, K to last 2 sts, SSK. 16 sts.
Row 54: SSP, P to last 2 sts, P2tog. 14 sts.
Row 55: K2tog, K to last 2 sts, SSK. 12 sts.
BO all sts and break yarn, leaving a 36" tail.

If you wish to use Insul-Bright thermal insulation fabric, use the inner layer as a template to cut a piece of the fabric.

Attach Inner Layer

Turn the outer layer inside out. If using Insul-Bright, lay cut piece over the full side (the side without the hole) of the pot grabber and pin in place. Lay the inner knit layer, RS facing, over top of the batting, sandwiching the batting in place. Using the long BO tail from the inner layer, whipstitch the inner layer to the WS of the outer layer.

Finishing

Weave in ends and turn right-side out.

Optional: An applied I-cord edge finishes off the piece. With the pot grabber flat, and starting in the middle of one straight edge, use Moroccan Red to work applied I-cord around the edge of the piece as follows. Graft final 3 sts to CO sts.

To work applied I-cord:

CO 3 sts. *Knit two stitches and slip the third stitch knitwise. PU and knit one more stitch from the edge. You will now have 4 stitches on your right needle.
Use your left needle tip to pass the slipped stitch over the last knitted stitch. This will leave you with three stitches on your right needle.
Slip these three stitches back onto the left needle tip, or slide to the other end of the needle, purlwise. Tug on the working yarn to tighten up the stitches.
Repeat these steps from *.

Weave in ends, and repeat for second pot grabber.

Pot Grabber Chart

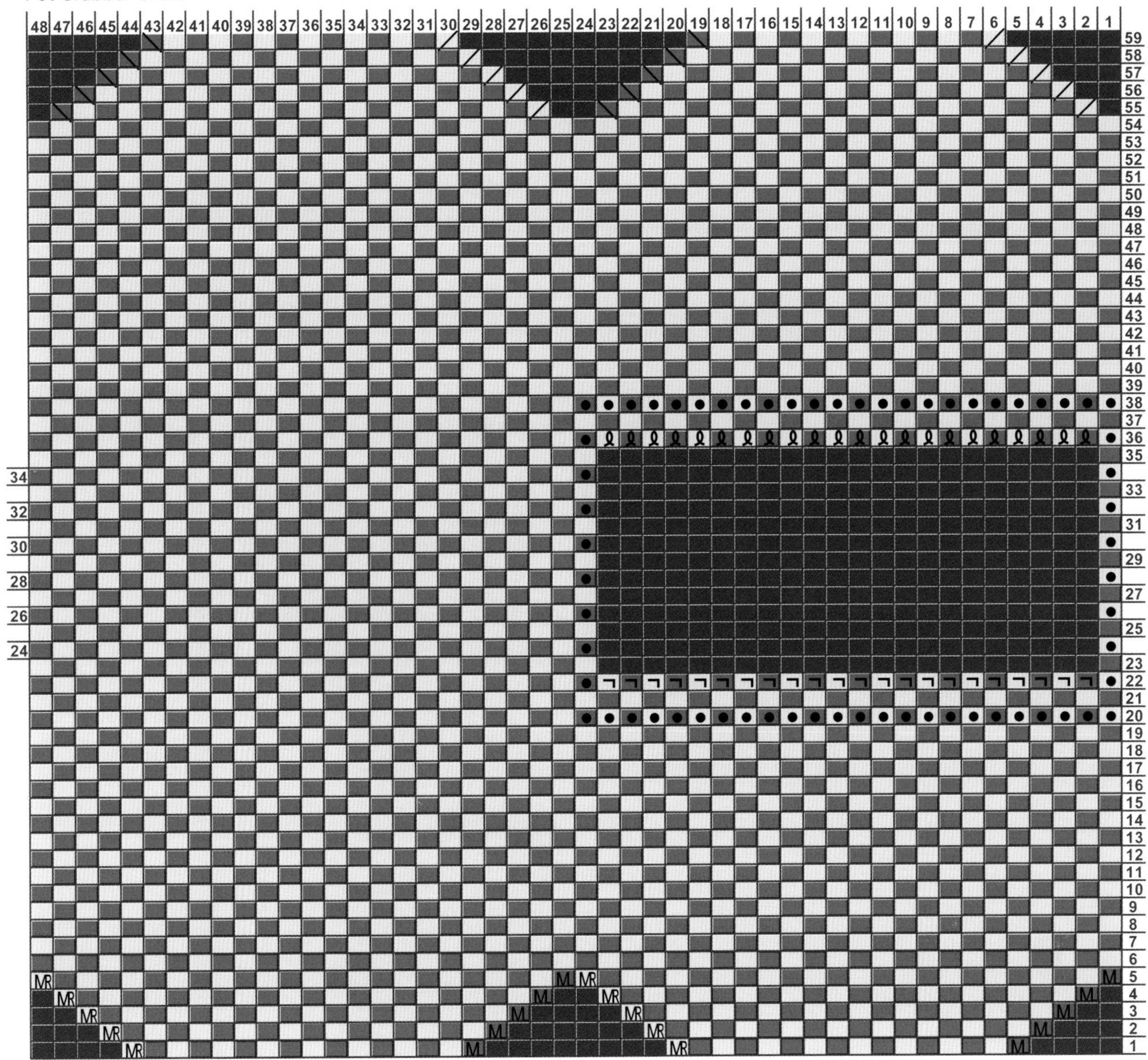

Work RS rows from L to R, and WS rows from R to L.While working from the chart, work with two colors at a time and carry the unused color up the inside.

Legend:

- No Stitch
- make one left
- RS: knit / WS: purl
- make one right
- RS: purl / WS: knit
- k2tog — Knit two stitches together as one stitch
- ssk — Slip one st as if to knit, Slip another st as if to knit. Insert LH needle into front of these 2 sts and K them together.
- Bind Off
- Cast On
- Swan
- Moroccan Red

SEED STITCH RUG

by Kerin Dimeler-Laurence

FINISHED MEASUREMENTS
48" long x 24" deep

YARN
Knit Picks Dishie (100% cotton; 190 yards/100g): MC Conch 25411, CC Fiesta Red 25786, CC1 Swan 25409, 4 balls each.

NEEDLES
US 15 (10 mm) straight or circular needles, or size to obtain gauge

NOTIONS
Large-eye Tapestry Needle
Crochet Hook and Scrap yarn for provisional CO
4 Stitch Markers

GAUGE
10 sts and 16 rows = 4" in Seed St, with yarn held tripled, blocked.

Seed Stitch Rug

Notes:

This squishy seed stitch rug is worked from the center out. Changing out one of the three strands held together every few rounds gives the rug an ombre effect, much like the braided rugs that inspired it.

Provisional Cast On (Crochet Chain method)

Using a crochet hook, make a slipknot and chain for 1". Hold knitting needle in left hand. With yarn in back of the needle, work next chain st by pulling the yarn over the needle and through the chain st. Move yarn under and behind needle, and repeat for the number of sts required. Chain a few more sts off the needle, then break yarn and pull end through last chain. CO sts will be incorrectly mounted; knit into the back of these sts. To unravel (when sts need to be picked up), pull chain end out, and the chain should unravel, leaving live sts.

M1 — PU the bar between st just worked and next st and place on LH needle mounted as a regular knit stitch; knit through the back of the loop.

M1 Pwise —Work as a make 1 increase, purling into the new st.

PFB — Purl into the front and back of the stitch.

DIRECTIONS

With crochet hook and scrap yarn, provisionally CO 60 sts. (Provisional CO can be worked in a single strand.) With MC held triple, (K1, P1) across all sts. Work in Seed St (knit the purls and purl the knits) for seven more rows. At the end of the last row, do not turn.

PM, PU and knit 4 sts down the adjacent short side of the work. Unravel provisional CO and place 60 sts on needles. PM and (K1, P1) across these sts; PM and PU and K 4 sts up the adjacent short side. PM for beg of rnd and join to work in the round; 128 sts.

Round 1: *(P1. K1) to next marker, SM, KFB four times, SM, repeat from *. 8 sts added; 136 sts.
Round 2: (K1, P1) around.
Round 3: *(P1, K1) to next marker, SM, P1, (K1, P1, K1) in next st, (P1, K1) twice, (P1, K1, P1) in next st, K1, SM; repeat from *. 8 sts added; 144 sts.
Round 4: As round 2.
Round 5: *(P1, K1) to next marker, SM, KFB, (K1, P1) to st before next marker, KFB, SM; repeat from *. 4 sts added; 148 sts.
Round 6: *(K1, P1) to marker, SM, K1, M1 Pwise, (K1, P1) to st before marker, M1, P1, SM, repeat from *. 4 sts added, 152 sts.
Round 7: *(P1, K1) to marker, SM, (P1, K1) 3 times, PFB, K1, P1, KFB, (P1, K1) to marker, SM; repeat from *. 4 sts added; 156 sts.
Round 8: Break one strand of MC, add one strand of CC. *(K1, P1) to marker, SM, (K1, P1) 3 times, M1, (P1, K1) 3 times, M1 pwise, (K1, P1) to marker, SM; repeat from *. 4 sts added; 160 sts.
Rounds 9-10: repeat rounds 5-6; 168 sts.
Round 11: *(P1, K1) to marker, SM, (P1, K1) 4 times, PFB, (K1, P1) 3 times, KFB, (P1, K1) to marker, SM; repeat from * to end. 4 sts added: 172 sts.
Round 12: Break one strand of MC, add one strand of CC. *(K1, P1) to marker, SM, (K1, P1) 4 times, M1, (P1, K1) 5 times, M1 Pwise, (K1, P1) to marker, SM; repeat from *. 4 sts added; 176 sts.
Rounds 13-14: Repeat rounds 5-6; 184 sts.
Round 15: *(P1, K1) to marker, SM, (P1, K1) 5 times, PFB, (K1, P1) 5 times, KFB, (P1, K1) to marker, SM; repeat from * to end. 4 sts added: 188 sts.
Round 16: Break final strand of MC, add one strand of CC. *(K1, P1) to marker, SM, (K1, P1) 5 times, M1, (P1, K1) 7 times, M1 Pwise, (K1, P1) to marker, SM; repeat from *. 4 sts added; 192 sts.
Rounds 17-18: Repeat rounds 5-6; 200 sts.
Round 19: *(P1, K1) to marker, SM, (P1, K1) 6 times, PFB, (K1, P1) 7 times, KFB, (P1, K1) to marker, SM; repeat from * to end. 4 sts added: 204 sts.
Round 20: Break one strand of CC, add one strand of CC1. *(K1, P1) to marker, SM, (K1, P1) 6 times, M1, (P1, K1) 9 times, M1 Pwise, (K1, P1) to marker, SM; repeat from *. 4 sts added; 208 sts.
Rounds 21-22: Repeat rounds 5-6; 216 sts.
Round 23: *(P1, K1) to marker, SM, (P1, K1) 7 times, PFB, (K1, P1) 9 times, KFB, (P1, K1) to marker, SM; repeat from * to end. 4 sts added: 220 sts.
Round 24: Break one strand of CC, add one strand of CC1. *(K1, P1) to marker, SM, (K1, P1) 7 times, M1, (P1, K1) 11 times, M1 Pwise, (K1, P1) to marker, SM; repeat from *. 4 sts added; 224 sts.
Rounds 25-26: Repeat rounds 5-6; 232 sts.
Round 27: *(P1, K1) to marker, SM, (P1, K1) 8 times, PFB, (K1, P1) 11 times, KFB, (P1, K1) to marker, SM; repeat from * to end. 4 sts added: 236 sts.
Round 28: Break final strand of CC, add one strand of CC1. *(K1, P1) to marker, SM, (K1, P1) 8 times, M1, (P1, K1) 13 times, M1 Pwise, (K1, P1) to marker, SM; repeat from *. 4 sts added; 240 sts.
Rounds 29-30: Repeat rounds 5-6; 248 sts.
Round 31: *(P1, K1) to marker, SM, (P1, K1) 9 times, PFB, (K1, P1) 13 times, KFB, (P1, K1) to marker, SM; repeat from * to end. 4 sts added: 252 sts.
Round 32: Break one strand of CC1, add one strand of MC. *(K1, P1) to marker, SM, (K1, P1) 11 times, M1, (P1, K1) 11 times, M1 Pwise, (K1, P1) to marker, SM; repeat from *. 4 sts added; 256 sts.
Rounds 33-34: Break one strand of CC1, add one strand of MC. Repeat rounds 5-6; 264 sts.
Round 35: *(P1, K1) to marker, SM, (P1, K1) 12 times, PFB, (K1, P1) 11 times, KFB, (P1, K1) to marker, SM; repeat from * to end. 4 sts added: 268 sts.
Round 36: Break final strand of CC1, add one strand of MC. *(K1, P1) to marker, SM, (K1, P1) 12 times, M1, (P1, K1) 13 times, M1 Pwise, (K1, P1) to marker, SM; repeat from *. 4 sts added; 272 sts.
Rounds 37-38: Repeat rounds 5-6; 280 sts.
Round 39: *(P1, K1) to marker, SM, (P1, K1) 13 times, PFB, (K1, P1) 13 times, KFB, (P1, K1) to marker, SM; repeat from * to end. 4 sts added: 284 sts.
Round 40: Break one strand of MC, add one strand of CC. *(K1, P1) to marker, SM, (K1, P1) 13 times, M1, (P1, K1) 15 times, M1 Pwise, (K1, P1) to marker, SM; repeat from *. 4 sts added; 288 sts.
Rounds 41-42: Break one strand of MC, add one strand of CC.

Repeat rounds 5-6; 296 sts.

Round 43: *(P1, K1) to marker, SM, (P1, K1) 14 times, PFB, (K1, P1) 15 times, KFB, (P1, K1) to marker, SM; repeat from * to end. 4 sts added: 300 sts.
Round 44: Break final strand of MC, add one strand of CC. *(K1, P1) to marker, SM, (K1, P1) 14 times, M1, (P1, K1) 17 times, M1 Pwise, (K1, P1) to marker, SM; repeat from *. 4 sts added; 304 sts.
Rounds 45-46: Repeat rounds 5-6; 312 sts.
Round 47: *(P1, K1) to marker, SM, (P1, K1) 15 times, PFB, (K1, P1) 17 times, KFB, (P1, K1) to marker, SM; repeat from * to end. 4 sts added: 316 sts. Break all strands of CC.
Round 48: Attach 3 strands of CC1. *Knit to marker, SM, K 30, M1, K 38, M1, K to marker, SM; repeat from *. 4 sts added; 320 sts.

BO all sts Pwise in CC1.

Finishing

Weave in all ends. Wash and block flat, stretching the rug into shape.

Knit Picks®

Knit Picks yarn is both luxe and affordable—a seeming contradiction trounced! But it's not just about the pretty colors; we also care deeply about fiber quality and fair labor practices, leaving you with a gorgeously reliable product you'll turn to time and time again.

This collection features

Dishie
Worsted Weight
100% Cotton

CotLin
DK Weight
70% Tanguis Cotton, 30% Linen

Curio
Lace Weight
100% Cotton

View these beautiful yarns and more at www.KnitPicks.com

Abbreviations

BO	bind off
cn	cable needle
CC	contrast color
CO	cast on
cont	continue
dec	decrease(es)
DPN(s)	double pointed needle(s)
EOR	every other row
inc	increase
K	knit
K2tog	knit two sts together
KFB	knit into the front and back of stitch
K-wise	knitwise
LH	left hand
M	marker
M1	make one stitch
M1L	make one left-leaning stitch
M1R	make one right-leaning stitch
MC	main color
P	purl
P2tog	purl 2 sts together
PM	place marker
PFB	purl into the front and back of stitch
PSSO	pass slipped stitch over
PU	pick up
P-wise	purlwise
rep	repeat
Rev St st	reverse stockinette stitch
RH	right hand
rnd(s)	round(s)
RS	right side
Sk	skip
Sk2p	sl 1, k2tog, pass slipped stitch over k2tog: 2 sts dec
SKP	sl, k, psso: 1 st dec
SL	slip
SM	slip marker
SSK	sl, sl, k these 2 sts tog
SSP	sl, sl, p these 2 sts tog
	tbl
SSSK	sl, sl, sl, k these 3 sts tog
St st	stockinette stitch
sts	stitch(es)
TBL	through back loop
TFL	through front loop
tog	together
W&T	wrap & turn (see specific instructions in pattern)
WE	work even
WS	wrong side
WYIB	with yarn in back
WYIF	with yarn in front
YO	yarn over